FROM DREAM, FROM CIRCUMSTANCE

Also by Douglas Worth

Of Earth, 1974
Invisibilities, 1977
Triptych, 1979

FROM DREAM

FROM CIRCUMSTANCE

New &
Selected Poems
1963-1983

by Douglas Worth

Apple-wood Books
Cambridge/Watertown

The author would like to thank the editors of the following publications in which some of these poems have previously appeared: *Aspect, The Aspect Anthology, The Boston Cyclist, The Colorado Quarterly, Creativities, Dark Horse, Fine Frenzy, (second edition, McGraw-Hill), The Guardian, The Harbor Review, The Henniker Review, The Lamp in the Spine, The Logic of Poetry (McGraw-Hill), Longhouse, Meadowbrook News Letter, The Nation, The Newton Library Anthology, New American Poetry (McGraw-Hill), The New Earth Review, The New Salt Creek Reader, The Newton Graphic, The Newton Teacher, The Newton Teacher's Quarterly, The Newton Times, New York Poetry, Nitty-Gritty, The Notre Dame English Journal, 100 Flowers Anthology, Poems & Pictures, Prologue, San Fernando Poetry Journal, Small Moon, The Sparrow Magazine, Trout Poems, Triptych, Visions, Whole Life Times, The Windflower Poetry Almanac,* and *Workshop.*

"Flashback" reprinted from the Massachusetts Review, copyright © 1966 by the Massachusetts Review, Inc.

"Sidewalk Duty" © 1969 by the New York Times Company, reprinted by permission.

"Maple" reprinted from Prairie Schooner, copyright © 1974 by the University of Nebraska Press.

"Kite" won first prize in the 1981 Sri Chinmoy Poetry Awards.

Of Earth, William L. Bauhan, publisher, 1974

Invisibilities, Apple-wood Press, 1977

Triptych, Apple-wood Press, 1979

The author would also like to thank the Artists Foundation, under the sponsorship of the Massachusetts Council on the Arts and Humanities, for the encouragement of a fellowship received during the writing of some of these poems.

From Dream, From Circumstance © 1974, 1977, 1984 Douglas Worth

ISBN: 0-918222-38-9

Phil

CONTENTS

Dreams to the Wind

OF EARTH

CUPID

An arrow has been driven into my heart.

When I try to wrench it out
it curls like a young vine
feathers and leaves dissolving
in my hand.

The days pass
into years.
Inside me I can feel something
healed over
slowly
flowering.

This happens
again
and again.

Once
prying open my chest
I found a nest
of throbbing
tarnished pearls.

Sometimes, just walking along
a green wind shivers
the meadows of my blood;
the air grows so lush and varied
I can hardly breathe.

EVE

About her ripeness hangs
palpable, aching to bruise.

Too close you could not breathe
you would have to crush all distance

until you felt that stain
of sweetness flood your bones

drowning in which you would drift
forever, lost, blessed, dust.

AFFAIR

The table cleared
she brings in coffee
and to make the bringing special
a ginger jar.

Empty
even of fragrance
it holds up
under the lamp

a childlike pattern
of blue and red
flowers
which we enjoy, imagining

not a meadow, but maybe
a sideporch garden
on an afternoon
without wind.

Come from her hands
for my delight
it fills up slowly
from inside.

We look on
in silence, sipping
at what
we can't say.

MARRIAGE

We could see it coming
on the horizon
a brightening

that rose, flawless
pointing
toward noon.

Lying, our eyes
half closed
in the meadow

its radiance
was too great
to look upon.

Veering, it left
a reflection, shaving
by which thin light

even the closets
we were going to paper
with roses fade.

SNAPSHOT

My thumb's pressure
in the tack, still holding

it curls
like an exhausted leaf

all but the features, still smiling, lost
and they a bit
distorted, as if suffering
the tension of being
committed too long to a passing
season

the eyes especially, those quick
naked creatures, caught by the flash
at the edge of their dark lives
ache
to be gone.

DIVORCE

For years the bones of some animal
lay rotting, wedged
somewhere inside the wall
of your smile.

Now all that's gone.
The professionals, who can do anything
have cleaned up
in time for lunch.
A fine dust settles over everything.

Still swallowing loose threads
of blood, paper roses, scraps of fresh cement,
you feel the side of your face
coming back
as through a thinning mist
the pain like an angry sun
begins to spread.

MAPLE

as if
burning
old love letters

one could empty the heart
of its weight
of yellowed dreams

and sleep
bone clean
and waken green

DEATH OF THE PAST

At home
more white stands out
in a room

a chair is scraped from the sun
a bowl brought out
then put away.

After a time
a stranger's clumsiness
the look of a day

invites us to believe
we have come far enough
alone, and to what end?

WHEN YOU COME INTO A ROOM

The season
does not change.

The flowers, leaning in vases
do not suddenly revive.

Yet, something
in the quality of light

shifting with the eyes' focus, heightening
to new acuteness

harmony
of air and object, motion and repose

becomes apparent
that was not

while you were in the hall
or on the stairs.

TOUCHING

husks of defeat
snarled logics
of denial
drawn slowly
under

the body a wakening
field
of desire
each bud, leaf tip, swollen
light films every edge

COMING

the contours of self
give way

clouding

as river
enters river

COCOONS AT THE WINDOW

All winter, ghostly
fists
of summer
they tapped the pane

crusted with a thick
glaze of snow
buried
a month ago

in our minds
another
promise that had not
borne fruit.

Tonight, floating
above the sill, the wings
still
tender with sleep begin

to stiffen, trembling
as when wind
shivers the skin
of a sail.

GIFT

My hand held out two plums
both swollen with sweet juice
one half-a-mouthful bigger.
We had been walking long
uphill, through dust and stone.

It was the slightest flicker
your hand made toward the one
in settling on the smaller
that let me know your thirst

the scarcely-broken arc
between pleasure and pleasure
that left me with a gift
beyond all measure.

ANNOUNCEMENT

Two nights ago
cradling packages
I dropped a fifth of Scotch
all over the driveway.

One picture shows a fish
with toes, another
an egg proceeding on course
through the left horn of a ram.

A poet, I'm supposed
to capture these things
and I try

but the images
nibble my fingers and scoot
the meanings swarm
off the page.

PENNY BALLOON

Two inches tall today
already stretching sleepy
miraculous fingers, toes
in your dark cradle, lined
with softest weaves of our love

even now, lulled in the warm
lap of your mother's blood
in your penny balloon you ride
beyond us, preoccupied
with all you must do to survive.

POEM FOR BROOKE/DADDY/DAD

You addressed your father as Father
complying with that strict male wish
for greetings, departures:
a faint peck on the lips—
like wolves, a kind of polite
throatbaring.

In high school, when I tried
lopping off Daddy to Dad
you went along.

Later, signing long family letters
from Africa, then Trinidad
full of the secret lives
of insects and birds
you had three labels to pick from
under Love.

Home, between marriages, for two days
I came down after a long, rough Christmas Eve
to find you alone
in the living room reading the funnies.
You rose as I came
wordlessly hugged you
kissed you on the mouth.

LOOKING AT HOUSES

Who is it running
through my head
from the door to that bush?

the living room, as we enter, in half-light
familiar
the heavily polished
piano, listening

upstairs, the master
bedroom, small for us, slightly
awesome
the door to the attic
cracked open

on the screened porch, someone has left
a pitcher of melting
ice cubes, mint faintly
breathing

the back yard a dream
of sunlight
and there
peering out from the roses
a stranger's face
with my eyes

PSYCHOLOGY OF LEARNING

Buried all afternoon in Hamachek's
Human Dynamics in Psychology and Education
I look up as Karen comes in
with three tomatoes from the garden.

Soaking my eyes, I sniff
their brilliant ripeness.

Christ! she has grown these
from that strip of dirt
by the garage.

Cleared, faintly luminous
I plunge back into
"The Deterioration in the Quality of Life Hypothesis."

A month from now
she'll walk in
and hand me you.

EVOLVING

here on my lap, as on some shore
at foam's edge, moist with darkness
life, new life
evolving, dimly casting about
in air

love, like new mountains
heaved out of the earth
above us, jagged, uncompromised
by the slow sculpturing
that follows birth

slate eyes, still muted
as the dawn
already the brightening
mystery draws you
on

BARRAGE

the constant weight, building
exhaustion

at 5 a.m. thumbs, pins and needles
the feeling you've got his arms on
wrongside out

the point when the quivering buzzsaw of his rage
spewing frayed nerves, grates bone—
when song, when even mother's breast
is no solace, the light gone sour . . .

"I keep thinking this will all be over
in a few days
so I can get back
to my life."

at the cleaners, remarking
"Well, it's only for the next eighteen years."
the white-haired, smiling lady replying
"Don't kid yourself, Mr. Worth—my boy's
thirty-four next week."

FATHER AND SON

1

Well, Colin, here we are
father and son
alone for the next hour or so
your tiny hands weaving, me at my rhyme
together obscurely borne
on the opalescent, brightening, darkening flow
of circumstance and time.

This morning at six
when I'd changed the latest sopping load
and was tucking you back
into the semi-darkness of your room
planning another hour's sleep for you
so I could do some work,
I suddenly realized I was seeing you
more as some thing I owned
to be picked up, admired, cleaned, and put away
than as a person with a life of your own
and no way of telling,
someone who, given the choice, might well prefer
not to go back to bed
if instead he could watch his daddy making coffee
letting the milk boil over, feeding the cats,
or just lie and look at the frosted window panes
sketching silvery angels around the green wine bottles,
and then come and watch me writing poetry.

2

I remember another study,
the heavy, closed atmosphere, intensity
of adulthood—so intriguing, awesome to me;
long walks through the South Indian dawn
all pearled about us, shimmering
sunbirds exploding from bush to bush,
coppersmiths in the high, molten leaves
hammering the new day . . .

so many things in this world
never wholly resolved—
growing, we tear ourselves
from dependence to independence,
from there to interdependence,
and it doesn't get any easier,
each stage ambivalent, incomplete
anxiety threading every bond of love—
and to say, as I did in another poem,
"We are one another
we must try not to turn
from ourselves,"
seems right to me still, and yet
we turn and turn
of Earth, unable to bear for long
the cold, the radiance of the sun.

3

The light is just becoming,
Karen sleeping two rooms away,
Bach softly flowing on and on.
Again I try to shape words to my life,
groping, beginning, along with you
who lie here amid the clutter of books and plants,
the rich disorder that surrounds my craft,
taking it all in, fussing a bit
when I leave you too long, until I must leave these lines
which have no meaning to you yet, and come
put my hand on you, talk to you, fix the covers, and look . . .

little other, little one
of us,
everyday you grow
both more and less incredible to me—
how must I seem to you
my head still swimming above you? maybe, each day
a little less unborn, more your newborn father.

SIDEWALK DUTY

Still half-asleep, a blur
of sound and light
the children mill about.

Their brightness wounds me—
I feel like an old man
my scarred hands brimmed with precious
seeds.

The bell scatters them
some to assume
a world created for their blossoming
some to hang back
like riches cast by the wind
on stony ground.

THE WHISTLE

Now it is autumn, scattering over the field
the children at football stop, face into the wind
wind clouding with leaves a moment
losing track of the ball, the goal undefended,
the teacher's whistle, the captain's cry of dismay
calling them back to the game's necessity.

If I were a boy again, I might pay no attention
to whistles and captains, when wind came up
and made a dark game of leaves,
but I turn my head
and blow the whistle, and blow it hard again
as if I could blow the leaves back into the trees.

PROFESSION

1

I teach
English at the Junior High Level
whatever that means

Robin, unfolding
leaf by leaf
Emily Dickinson's seared
luminous heart

2

2000 tons of bombs dropped yesterday
the Red River Delta
running blood
"to preserve America's honor
from stain"

"Kontum will be saved
even if that means
the city's total destruction."

America, how can I stop you
from burying Vietnam
or your elected officials
from desecrating the language
day after day for savage ends?

A poet, I make
a living trying to teach
a handful of your children
something of that labor
toward clarity
which is no instant

recipe for action
but an attitude
demanding what is
ultimately, perhaps
unwarranted faith and courage
faced with the maze
the mystery
of the world.

3

Dianne's "We know our world
of imaginary beauty
has failed us."

Keith's "There was nothing on TV
but I watched anyway."

Sharon's *To President Nixon:*
"Sir, do you call cemeteries
peace?"

Julie's "Will the pieces ever fit?
I think they've started
But how do I keep them together?
Tape?
Glue?
No, something stronger
Love."

ICARUS

Below him now in the distance
he saw the diminished figure
turn and come wheeling back

too late
the wings molted
as the young man

exulting, on his own
at last, began
the dizzying plunge.

WAR BRIDE

Clear nights, the massive
drone of planes—
curled on the mat, she hugs
her breasts, singing
over and over, something
about the shining
of new pots.

This morning a letter.
She gathers herself
to read, holds it
unopened:
writing this, he
was alive
his spit in the glue.

AFTER THE HOMECOMING

kept going
by his dream of her
pining
or fed up, even, forgivably
unfaithful,
at any rate, a woman
toward whom he must strive
continually, against diminishing odds

seeing himself
as the hero, passing through, slaying
his quota of monsters, surviving
a goddess' arms, a trek
through the land of the dead

arriving, therefore
totally unprepared
for her strength
the impenetrable dream she had woven
of him as the tide-broken wanderer
herself the haven

what remained of the past
between them, that first night
rousing stiffly
to wag its tail once and die

after the homecoming horns had faded away
left facing each other
ceremoniously at the long table
like guests who have outstayed their stories

like ships drifting crippled
unable to meet
unable to release each other

he mooning down by the shore again
she slowly mounting
the smoothed stone steps to her window
the wreck of her loom

VEZELAY

Richard, lion heart
come
to lay your sword at Christ's feet

didn't you tremble
hesitate
here, at the last

judgment
where the slaughtered
lamb turns executioner?

EXCAVATION

always
here and there
in the rubble
among the fallen
wheels, helmets, shattered
stone limbs, heads

the delicate
flaming
of a leaf, a girl's sex
millenniums ago
still flickering
from the charred page

in porcelain, gesso, crazed
that apple blossom
milkiness
of a baby's temple

unwearying
flower of light

POEM ON MY THIRTY-THIRD BIRTHDAY

Watching you
drift now

folded
into me

my cradling arm in the soft
flow of your hair

beautiful

the blood still blooming
fading
from your cheek

I cannot sleep.

a son
a house now, land
of our own

Living
in evil times
evil, as I imagine all times
must be evil, and good
beyond reckoning

what does it mean to be
"responsible
adults"?

my presents
waiting
in the living room

seed packets, tools

under the painful gloss
of perfect fruits and flowers
the fine mysterious dust

the shovel
leaning heavily
in the darkness
pointing
its blade to the earth

INVISIBILITIES

QUEST

always
about to arrive
elsewhere
than this
obviousness, imagining
marvels unfolding
the sudden
transfiguring slant

surrounded
by the familiar
landscape of things as they are
where one might concede
at any point, finding oneself
in the present, eternally
flowering, withering moment, the fabulous
unredeemed here and now

SELF-PORTRAIT: WRITING

Beginning in darkness
I see myself

obscurely
in the window

become with the light
the world.

WORLDS
(for William Bronk)

Being here
we go on as if
it makes sense

this precarious, wild
sometimes painfully
beautiful act

we perform
over and over, whirling
through space

of tearing down, building
from chaos, order
a home—

those before us, after us
tearing down, building
again

imperfect, fictions
all, yet part
of the one

that has made us
what we are
as if through us

the world is trying
to make sense
of itself.

THE SUMMER HOUSE
(for Viki)

He never asked
preferring
not to know
why the church bell below his terrace
chimes the hours twice
leaving a timeless space
of silence in between—
the first few days
new to the country
he had thought it strange
that time upon these hills
should seem to stop

but hour circling hour
days, months, years
the fact became a welcome
ritual
part of the rhythm
of his laboring
pressed slowly on his mind
till it became symbolic
of a life
that might have been
conceived in Eden
once between a time.

Now, through the rich
late August afternoon,
a text, notebooks
a newspaper from home
spread on the table

where he sits at work,
he feels the year recede
the slanting light
upon him like a weight
indifferent
to all his years
have still to undertake.

A sudden bell breaks
inward on his thought,
another—vision blurs:
the warm green hills
caught in a flood
of light and music, rise:
above, circling
on weightless wings, a hawk
carves azure endlessly
till time itself
unravelling air and bone
must catch its breath.

Vesancy, France

VESANCY

mornings, the windows
are doors, opening
inward

the mind in that light
washed naked, we enter
as children

a landscape whose objects
in their first freshness
come nuzzling our senses

one after one
to be named

FLASHBACK
(for Mother and Dad)

the strawberries
that summer, lasted forever
and the apple trees always
blossoming, dropping and bending,
huge swallowtails gracefully
flitting from nets we flung

and the long evenings, voices
of grown-ups drifting in bursts
from the moonlit lawn
mysterious, muffled
as moth wings colliding, buzzing
against the screen

GUESTS IN EDEN
(for Ellen)

sun-lazing, mornings
looking out
from the high terrace
it is as if
one has not asked too much
has earned
these few weeks, guests in Eden

yarrow sloping to meadow
ash and oak
a village
patchwork of farmland rolling beyond
to a city, too distant to touch us
decorative,
in the sheltering mountains
mille fleurs walks

but a letter, in dreams
another world encroaching . . .

what they could see
from the rose-clouded fence:

the animals, flowering
antler, crest, and mane
opposed, proud, violent
slaughtering one another

slow-paced and courtly
the same creatures, caught
in the inextricable
pageant of desire—

inside them, countering
all that peace
to the less and less containable need
to reach out and touch, to know
whatever is . . .

our own ambivalence, taking leave
of the dove-filled trees
the streams, endless windings
through bluebells and raspberries
suggesting what pain
they suffered, as they turned
to meet the unknown
dimly advancing fall

RETURN

The *Times* feels heavy, day
skids by on squealing rubber
nothing has changed
but flashes

inside us, stars
that still appear
so close our hands
might brush them away

flooding the subway, fields
where we lay and fed
each other's mouths ambrosial
wine and bread

DEER CROSSING
(for Karen)

there
where we've put a road through
and put up a sign

we encounter
the problem

of our being
both in and out
of nature

indifferent
and responsible
to her laws

though for the most part we manage
to avoid it

sometimes at night
the blind eyes, the machine
interpenetrate

"THE SMALL NOUNS"
(for George Oppen)

bird
in the sense of wonder
and recognition

and therefore
an anguished
sense of oneself

alive, among fellow
creatures, precariously
acting and exposed

in a world
of flowering
metals, singing

bird
in the sense
of prayer

SNOWDROPS

exposing, this morning
white tips so fragile
they bruise in the wind

do not mistake them

whose ancestors gauged
eons of granite
and yoked the wild sun

SLAP

mountainous, the ancient
tyranny of the big
as against the need, real need
for law . . . crumbling

my hand reaching out
to find you, afraid
which you took, as if a branch
of olive . . . gathering

lifting you, safe
safe, safe, little love, a wonder
any of us survives

SEA-CHALLENGER
(for Marc)

Knee-deep in swirling foam
lips curling, clenched fists raised
you watch the breakers glide
and build till they loom like walls
that towering pitch and plunge
crashing against your chest.

Little sea-challenger
sand caving under your feet
how can you stop the waves
that can wrestle oaks to the ground
as they slowly crush and grind
mountains to glittering dust?

But to take such a stance, to feel
muscle and bone and will
bracing, as shock after shock
you meet that relentless thrust
spray dazzling your eyes, on your tongue
the salt of life strong and sweet!

EAGLE

When the ungainly brood
are of an age

he leads them
up to thin bare boughs

and abandons them
to flop in the wind

hiding himself
on a low branch upstream

where for weeks unflinching
he watches the sky

for panic and hunger to toughen
their reluctant sinews

then drives them screaming
into their lives.

GROWN-UP

like when you find yourself
looking around and asking
"Who the fuck's in charge here?"
and it's you

SKIN FLICK

because the alternative
is hard, is almost too much
the risk: pierced, swept off, sliding

to the verge of self, beyond, where
luminous, blossoming
no word for it: "love," "I love you"
missing, the charged air flickering
the moment withering, leaving us
exposed, raw, shrinking
back, out
of the garden
of each other . . .

this
reduction, these bodies
consumers, anonymous
meat

THE GOD, THE GODDESS

1

Before them, blurred, distorted
is the image
of two lovers they've never seen before
who don't seem to know themselves
or each other either
as they hammer and gobble
one another's bodies
blindly, their flesh on the cheap film
stained by a light
that seems itself wounded, raw
until, in some bleak charade
of consummation
gravy of semen slithers
down her chin.

2

Before them, standing together
bathed in the light
of oil lamps, flickering
a deep blue-green
fragrance of forest
flowers around his neck,
he is dark, and radiant, fathomless
ocean, jewel, his flute resting
lightly in one hand, the other
clasping her
whose beauty is softer
more fluid, a river
of gold.

They begin to sing
of his flute, its infinite
tenderness, longing, power
searching the meadows, calling
compelling her,
the loveliness of her dancing
each gesture, glance
delicate and quick
as a lightning flash,
the dark and gold of their trembling
bodies flowing together
mingling, blurred

3

One rises from the crowd
stands a moment, rocking
starts to weave
past faces turning along the aisle,
suddenly staggers, whirls, his eyes
glazed, a green glitter,
balances, whirls again
and, like some ancient
genius of the place
calling out darkly
to the god, the goddess,
stretches his arms wide
and begins to dance.

MUSE

When you come carelessly
naked from the shower
passing from room to room
shaking out your hair

what can I do
but follow

while something of that
cast-off radiance flows
gathers, and flows again
down the blank page.

ORPHEUS, TURNING

not out of doubt

to release her, both
no longer of either world

the blood ore
in his veins, her eyes flowering
diamonds, waiting for him

to turn and plunge blindly
into the alien
light

LOVERS

all of us
writhing, caught
in the world's embrace, each other's
dreams and shit on our hands

DA NANG

in the dream I would have done anything
to stay alive

face, our face, we have seen it
before, and now in living color, barbarous
face of the human
machine breaking down

walking through woods I thought
I am leaf, rock, in the wind
it is enough

it is not enough

CHRISTMAS

the children
under the illumined tree

bombarded
scrambling out, shrieking
for us to see

our gifts
ablaze in their hands

REPUBLIC

what had been conceived
as a land
ruled by the people
growing, becoming

confused
by size, sheer number
the machinery grinding, advancing
out of hand

lives mangled
the people receding, caught
in the relentless logic
of their own success

in the wake of empire
bands
of the saved, the eroded
going under, turning

inward, back
to the simple, eternal
light
in the Orient

LINCOLN TO JFK

Does it bloom
in every dooryard, brother
lifting sweet petals to each shower
and after, fragrance so rich
when the clusters brush your cheek
it stuns the breath?

Or does that dream still lie
mutilated, wasted, torn
roots and leaves drifting
in another flood
of statesmen's rhetoric
and soldiers' blood?

DREAMERS

who ached beyond
mere drudgery of subsistence
urging the possible
a little further
than at first it had wanted to go

THE TASK

one day the clear task
unfolding, dazzling, immense
vision piercing the heart
of a horizon so vast even death
would be a kind of success

then months, years of this slogging
through piled snow, leaves, where the path
keeps losing itself in brambles, and whatever
that voice up ahead is calling, it is not
the sea! the sea!

MICHELANGELO

a little man
disfigured
imagine

the beautiful people
in the parks, public gardens
crowded, at dusk

his dwarfish figure
among them, shouldering home
paint-spattered, searching each gesture

his room, the mirror avoided
before sleep the dim ceiling
swarming with gods

ELEGY
(for Rainer Maria Rilke)

Beginning, on your own
even as a child
you found words
playing hide-and-seek
with things.

Not so much alone
as elsewhere, out of touch
with the others at their games,
missing the ball
you leapt for the sun instead
sinking beyond the fingers
of the trees—
and you found words
that caught the fall
of things.

In class, when they asked for dates
of battles, kings
you gave them the circling
eagles behind time's eyes
and bared a glittering era
with a phrase—
for you found words
that stripped the rind
from things.

Drifting through the conventions
of the days and years,
mealtimes, jobs, fashions, cities
happened to you
though you had trouble remembering

directions, names, and the latest
news never took you
where you wanted to go—
but you found words
that sipped the juice
of things.

One day, you sucked the heart
out of a rose;
once the deep singing
marrow from an oak;
one night a girl
burst on your tongue
like a burning seed—
you had found words
that plunged to the core
of things.

Unsatisfied, your thirst
for discovery grew so great,
abandoning Earth, you soared
up to the dim cathedral
of the heavens;
advancing, star by star
you sensed the invisible
presence of awesome powers
pervading, ordering, binding
the universe,
and called them angels, beyond us
flowing in pure
unalterable perfection
as veins through alabaster
next to those
threading the softer white
of a woman's wrist—

and you found words
that bowed before the mystery
of things.

Chastened, you returned
to the familiar
seamless face of things,
letting them dwell and be
inside you, shining
more sweetly for their corrupt
mortality—leaf, wing, stone
transfigured, radiant, each
a little sun,
that had not been
and never would be again,
caught up by forces, flung
on some fathomless journey
blindly, each in its time
adding irrevocably
its tiny sum
to the infinite
flowing of eternity—
and you found words
that praised
the passing-in-everlastingness
of things.

One day they came, lamenting
that you had died
and bore away a shell
and were satisfied,

but you had left them the living
fruits of your eyes
for all who would come

and like you, reaching, try
the mingled tastes of Earth
and paradise,
and gone on ahead—
and you found words
that were not words for things
translations, but things themselves
speaking their native tongues,
and became one with them
beginning again.

Vesancy—Muzot—Raron

OTHER

looms on the horizon, radiant
angel or demon
of infinite possibility advancing

till half-blinded, trembling, limbs aching
to turn, to reach out
new leaves

we stand gazing beyond
whatever we are
or were

BREAKTHROUGH

that shiver
and flood of wreckage
light, the blind
beak piercing the shell

FOUNTAIN

from dream, from circumstance, what we try
to make of ourselves—that fountain
in the cemetery, the ragged jet
splashing down to the basin, gathered
in a moving stillness, spilled over
clear threads twisting windblown
the chipped stone scattering beads

the art, the disappearing
act of life

TRANSFIGURATION
(for Val)

piecemeal, the world
is falling
in through the holes
of the body
filtered
by the mind and heart
down to that dark
dense core

which opens, or closes
in hunger, sated
nourished, battered
responding, avoiding

riots and roses, sparrows
Mozart, potatoes, murders
crabgrass and lovers

the debris
of days, rotting
scraps of information

sifting, dissolving

elephants, fashions, philosophers
toppling
whole cities crumbling
wars, generations, breakthroughs
pouring in
through the cracks

compressed
silting down

the weight of it
growing, the pressure
building

the small self struggling
to absorb, to escape

and there is no way
out

old civilizations
drifting, the dust, the dreams
of millennia
galaxies

relentlessly
pressing in

till it cannot be borne
or resisted
another minute
everything
collapses
caves in
goes black

black

black

no

something

is beginning
to happen

down there
in the dark

something

has cracked
a crust
seed
spark
flickering
deep
at the crux

is lifting
unfolding
frail
petal-feathers
of light

look

it is the world
transfigured, rising
a new, fragrant
jewel, singing
star

TRIPTYCH

THE SEVENTH DAWN

He is still sleeping
peacefully, his face
turned toward the brightening, gleams
as if with its own dim light
as I approach.

So like a god
immaculate, he seems
almost too perfect
for mortality,
his rose mouth fit for hymns
of near-angelic
harmony and grace,
yet sensual, keen
with its lush slidings, chiseled teeth
for the more savage work
of animals.

Curled on themselves, his hands
like petals, acorns
gathering force—
what acts
of infinite precision, reach
ordering chaos
holocaust, may spring
out of their delicate
awakening?

I smooth a curl back
brush the silky bloom
of his warm, sleep-flushed cheek—
his eyes flicker open
blindly, close, absorbed

in dreamwork, bloodwork
flowing beyond my grasp
around the bones
that will support the flowering
of his life
a little while, then fold
and crumble back
to the unconscious
dust from which they rose.

Drawn down by love and fear
for what I have created
in my own image, grown
mysterious and distant
on his own,
ignorant, helpless, and responsible
I bend and gently plant
upon his brow a trembling
kiss of choice.

THIS

unquestioned
unquestioning
mostly, as one cannot
stop and gape
always

reflecting in the middle
of the street, as the light
changes, must
get on with the business
of making it
across

cannot hesitate
to consider
the mysterious
beautiful
lips open, glistening
hungrily
to be filled
with light, cock, meat, drink, air

yet, moments
of awareness, wonder
that it's all here
that we are, somehow
happening, the privilege
unlooked for
wonderful, terrible
miracle

of this

GODFATHER

tough customers, Americans.

"We're gonna make you
an offer
you can't refuse."

a businesslike
ethic
of power

at work
in Manhattan
at Kontum
Wounded Knee

that has permeated
so much
of all we have accomplished

and proven
in terms of what we have
dreamed of
as a people, venomous

REVOLUTIONARY AGENDA
(for Tom)

what one must do
to make it
in one's field

and what
to make it
through the night

a land
where these two thorny blossoms
intertwine

HOSPITAL WINDOW

1

oranges, forsythia
bloom on the sill

2

mornings, the brightly colored
numberless little cars with their urgent
purposefulness
glide along the river's edge

all afternoon raindrops
merge, jostling blindly
down the pane

at midnight the gleaming
hives of industry,
a red light
like a pulsing ache:
Time, Temperature
Coca-Cola

3

oasis
Olympian calm
in the midst of feverish
progress

from which a dizzying
perspective
of what is of importance
should we return . . .

to rescue, somehow
something . . . a leaf, going under
the relentless wheel

4

rising at dawn to lean
above the river
returning slowly, dim
as health

drawn by the gulls'
restless circling

there is fear in the question
of what it means
to get well

MOMENTS

flesh blooming
bathed
in a soft shimmering
nimbus

dimmed
by the conflicting
desires, demands, limitations
of mortality

blighted, obscured
by the expedient
abuses, perversions
of this or that system
we suffer, come to think of
as our lives

as if there were no mystery
no miracle
in the clear fact
that we are here, living together
that we are here at all

under the familiar
husk
the live kernel
smoldering
suddenly blazing
out of the dark

MARY

a window
open
so wide
stretching, she burst
into blossom,
light's touch made her heavy
with ripeness

so that the ghostly radiance
spreading its seed
inside her, for a moment
could not distinguish
her flesh from its grace
was just barely able
to tear itself out, reascend

THE ANGEL TO JOSEPH

As when
amid strewn shavings
and bent nails
some spirit of grace
surpassing thought or skill
informs your patient laboring
prevails
until the work stands finished
luminous
and you drop, humbled, dumb

she is God's work,
and kneels in awe
to her own glory.

Come!

THE WISE MEN

Stiff from kneeling
on the cold earth floor
we rise, groaning, stretch and yawn
reclaim our crowns
and set out into the dark
from which we came

gossiping, swapping jokes, flasks, anxious
to resume the familiar
traffic of the world
where our word is law

relieved to let fade
for the moment, the miracle
of incarnation
taking place in the midst
of animal noises, smells,
our bowed gray heads
charged with radiance
jeweled with blood,
spirit flooding the body's confines
like a star.

2 WALKING

everywhere lethal
treasure—I said, "Careful
put that down, that's dirty, that
could cut you, those
will make you sick."
he said, "Look
at this one, what's this one
Dada, oo, well I want to
bring this one home."

THE MEANING OF LIFE
(for Jim McDade)

at least that's the lofty title
of the poem I set out to write
this morning at 6:30
based on a dream I'd just had
that seemed to be saying it all

I'd just settled down in the kitchen
at my favorite writing place
the table by the window
with its two or three flowering plants
(the window still full of darkness
the plants looking half asleep)
and was sipping coffee and smoking
my second cigarette
having been interrupted
already a number of times
by Tiggy's comings and goings
(when he's in and wants to go out
his claws in your thigh let you know it
when he's out and wants to come in
he lunges at the screen door
and hangs there, spread-eagled, yowling
till someone takes pity on him)
but anyway, I'd settled down
and had actually written the title
and was zeroing in on my dream
when the swinging door swung open
and in walked Colin, my son

O shit! there goes my poem
I thought, but what could I do?
he's four years old, and I love him

and he loves me, in spite of the fact
(or is it *because* of the fact?)
that we're caught up together in this
incredible family thing
that tears along at a clip
of a zillion miles per second
most of the time we're awake
with rarely a thank you or please

so in he came, in his pajamas
all smiles, and wanting to sit
at the other end of the table
and spend some time with me

I told him about the work
I had to do, mentioned the poem
(he knows that I do that
though he doesn't really know
what poetry's all about
not that I'm so sure myself)
and said, "Why don't you go get a book
or I'll give you a pen and some paper
and we can work here together
wouldn't that be fun?"

but he didn't take to that
so we just sat there awhile
making faces and bits of talk
half serious, half silly
the way we often do
when nothing special's up
and he'd brought his twirly thing
we got yesterday at the circus
that lights up and makes a soft

low whistling sort of moan
when you pull the strings and it spins
so he was showing that off

and after a while, as it seemed
he wasn't about to move on
I poured juice and made him some cocoa
between hot and warm, with the spoon
left in the cup, as he likes it
and we sat and talked some more
about one thing and another
like why such and such is true
and how come this and that?
and what would you do if?
and can wolves or weasels jump
as high as a second-floor window?
and what do trees think about?
and I could feel my poem
slowly circling the drain

well, at some point I made up my mind
and told him I had to work
and that he could go see Mommy
or play in the living room
his bedroom, or the basement
but, in short, that he had to clear out
all very calm and friendly
but firm, and he'd picked up
his twirly thing in one hand
and his other was rubbing one eye
when he said casually, "Dada
do your eyes sometimes start to water
when nothing's hurting them?"

I said, "Sure they do, sometimes sleep
gets gunky stuff in your eyes
and makes them water a bit
when you wake up and start to rub them."

then he said something else
I couldn't catch, but his voice
had gone a bit thick and wobbly
and he was trying to clear it
again and again, with no luck
and I was suddenly listening
and looking at him hard
and finally I said, "Colin
are you feeling a little bit sad?"

his reply was all gunked up
so I said, "Why don't you come over
and sit here on my lap
and we'll get all cozy and warm."
so he brought his juice and cocoa
without spilling a single drop
and we sat there, rocking and rocking
not saying anything much
sort of blooming, along with the plants
and then the window was light
and Tiggy was yowling again

so we let him in and went up
and I washed and shaved and got dressed
and he went in to see Mommy
and then I drove off to work
thinking I'll try that poem
during my free block at school
if I can remember the dream

I can't but I've still got the title
so this poem, if that's what it is
will have to do, and maybe
it's closer to the truth
about the meaning of life
(if there is such a thing) than any
a dream could have given me

READING X

Stunned
by that bleak, unsparing
honesty
in poem after poem

that drives home the brutal
day you've just had at work
where nothing went right

your memory coughs up everything
you ever tried
to forget

failures
of parents, friends, lovers, marriage, fatherhood
agonies
of childhood, growing up, sliding
through an aimless, indifferent universe
in terror, toward the abyss

the unreclaimable
disaster areas
of your character
that disappoint even the cat!

"Jesus!" you groan.
"He's got me
by the balls—I admit
to everything!"

Scourged of illusion
taking what's left of your life
naked in shaking hands

you drag home under a darkening sky
of unrelieved anguish, despair
to find the house empty of those
who are supposed to love you
and sit down to write it all out
spewing image on image
of bottled-up misery, spleen
in the kitchen, glumly preparing
for them to come back and find you
purged, immaculate, bone!

They arrive from shopping
first your older son,
four-and-a-half, unaware
as yet, of the change,
comes barreling, breathless, in
to demonstrate the new padlock
and chain he's got for his bike
he's just learning to ride
without the training wheels,
shakily balancing
as you run alongside to catch him

next the younger, the easy one
drifts in, in one sock, mumbling
a phrase from a silly song
you sang him the other night
when he seemed more asleep than awake,
and wants a big hug and a kiss
and a handful of Cheddar Cheese Goldfish

then your wife, whose shortcomings
would make an imposing list
almost as long as your own

if you set your pen to it,
sweeps in and lofts you a kiss
over the shopping bags
one of which has a giant erection
of Italian bread sticking out
that goes with your favorite dinner
of steak and garlic butter,
and not only fails to remark
the new, *real* you sitting there
but sounds more resigned than angry
when she points out the pellets of mud
you've tracked unthinkingly
again, on her kitchen floor

and seeing her, you remember
the movie that's on at nine
you're both planning to watch,
and that it's been 3 or 4 nights
since you've made love, and how good
how *goddam* good her ass looks
for a woman of thirty-four
who's borne you two sons, kept house
and on with her career
part-time, rearranging her life
so cheerfully around
the demands of a family
and you and your moody muse
for what is it now? nine years?
and how you'd promised her
to change the Kitty Litter
this afternoon, for sure!

And later, after you've scoured
the litter pan, bagged the trash

read 5 books, aborted 3 fights
been screamed at, fled from in tears
ambushed, ridden, devoured
resurrected, tickled, abandoned
for dinner, to lie on the couch
like the contemplative
eye of a hurricane
jotting down scraps of a new
poem that's starting to come
at just the wrong time, drawn baths
smoothed tangles, wrestled pajamas
spun a yarn from the on-going saga
of Karl the Kingfisher
(who spears 2 tin cans, a milk carton
3 leaves and a baseball cap
before finally landing a fish—
being, from birth, afflicted
with blurred vision, a fear of heights
and too much imagination,
yet struggling heroically
and generally managing
through it all, to hang on to his senses
of humor and perspective
as he gets up and goes to work
and returns to the clamoring nest
rain or shine, each day of the week)
tucked in both Snoopies, bent
in the half-lit hush to give
and receive the warm, moist, living
mystery of a kiss

as you're plowing through the strewn chaos
of pillows and toys and books
in the living room, downing a Scotch
digging Peterson, smelling the steak

already savoring
that pungent, buttery mess
sloshing around in your mouth

it suddenly strikes you that X,
for all his uncompromising
ferocious honesty
in flaying life to its nerves,
has missed an essential point
which needs to be made, about sharing
commitments, obligations
and working hard to support
each other, as best we can,
not just in those desperate times
of gloom, when the sun appears
to swing like a bloodied ax,
but through that ambivalent haze
of less spectacular
conflicts, triumphs, concessions
anxieties, needs, satisfactions
etc., that make up the bulk
of the day-to-day, long-term haul
we're all caught up in together
until the world fades and we
relinquish all storms of light

and how little X admits
of that other extreme: those moments
that come with a piercing rush
of tenderness, joy, love, grace,
whatever it is that fills you
till, brimming, you want to shout
obscenities at the stars
or smother the cat with kisses,
though you don't, as you might wake the kids

or get clawed in the face for your pains—
you just sweep up the plastic trash bag
that's waiting for you by the door
and growling, "Come here, you sweet thing!"
boogie out into the night.

INVITATION

nothing one can do
is ever going to be
enough, whether
as son, lover, drudge, parent, guardian
of the Word, the world
keeps coming around
for more, someone is always raiding
the fridge, or trying to
start something or dropping
hints or dead at one's feet, and time is not
on one's side—therefore take care
to love yourself
not least, let the world look after itself
now and then, buy an ice cream, settle back
with a cold beer, take in
a game, get into the swing
of that ass, the sweet breasts
of roses, after all, one is only
human, a puff
of elevated dust, in that shaft
of sunlight the ancestral
bones are dancing

EASTER

Nothing. Good.
We are lost
and therefore free

to begin again
creating out of corrupt
mortality, a vision

of universal
kinship
in which light

each caring act
would outshine
the indifferent stars.

DREAMS TO THE WIND

ONCE I WANTED TO SAVE THE WORLD

by writing poems of global consciousness
but wherever I went the world objected
to my style, the fuzziness
of my thinking, my simplistic
prognoses, prescriptions, the sluggish, abstract prose
of my rhetoric, the insufferable arrogance
of my savior's posture, hinting around that at forty
with a wife, 2 kids, a house, turtle, cats, a dog
named Rover, tenure at twenty-two thousand a year
and a taste for Scotch and Sunday afternoon football
I'm too comfortably off and conventionally set to start
any kind of revolution—in short
the world didn't seem to want to be saved
at least by me, so I said, "O.K., fuck it!" and turned back
to the funnies and flowers
and TV and sex and making a buck and fooling
around with the kids and the dog and helping out
with the housework that never gets done and keeping up
with a few friends and colleagues and coming to terms
with my personal failings and the steady recession
toward nothingness of my hairline and the fact
that this whole business of life, awareness and choice
adds only the faintest trace of sweet and sour
to the otherwise tasteless flow
of eternal cosmic oblivion—and I tried
to stop worrying about the world
that didn't want me to save it, and just be
a poet who writes for himself and God
and submits to *The New Yorker*—but it's hard
to completely forget how once you wanted
to save the whole fucking world
when, despite everything, you still do

and wherever you go you hear, "Save me!"
"Save me!" "Save me!" till you say
"O.K., I'll try, but don't expect too much
and remember, this time you asked for it, didn't you?
didn't you?"

NO!

Because the horror
and suffering
would be

beyond anything
we can grasp
and no image could touch

the sheer waste and loss
of so much
we and nature have tried,

approach some small commonplace
tangible thing
like a flower

and bending
to take in its loveliness
become

for a moment
petaled and open
languorously

spreading your fragrant
silkiness
to the sun,

and in the midst
of blossoming
feel yourself suddenly

flare, crumple, feather
and scatter
as ashes forever—

then try to come back
from that shriveling
instant of vision

without saying No!

THE TRUTH ABOUT WAR

As only survivors
come back to talk about it
and having just visited
they don't really count

if you want to get closer
to the truth about war
seek one who stayed on
forever—go down

past chiseled
abstractions, gnawed
boards, fraying
cloth and skin

to where worms are quietly
tearing the lips
from the non-partisan
friendliness of the grin

and see if the echo
of anthem, shriek, or moan
ruffles that fixed neutrality
of bone.

CHECKPOINT

Make way for the great
wildly-elbowing
human race

running blindly
out of energy
time and space

toward the finish
where there will be laurels
and baskets of sweet

deformed, starving babies
strewn
at the victors' feet.

"THIS LAND IS YOUR LAND

for as long as grass shall grow
and water flows"

you promised
in writing
a century ago

but the yellow
metal that makes you
crazy was stronger.

Now the blue-playing rivers
you harnessed lie blackened
in pools, or crawl barren
in chains through the broken
hearts of a thousand cities

the grass has gone under
a crazy golden
ocean of greed flowing over
the bones of the green-waving prairies
you cleared for your harvest.

This land
is *your* land now, truly, the old broken
promise fulfilled.

THE BIG APPLE

Somewhere, buried
at the core
of all that incredible
crush of stone, steel, glass
and living flesh

a little girl
is eating
strawberry shortcake
on the uptown
double-A train

whipped cream
all over her chin,
grinning back at two strangers,
and calling out, "Mira!
Mira!"

to her father
who is gazing
down at the big apple
of his dreaming
eye.

BIKING TO WORK

The birds are still out there
singing at 7:30
to beat the band, the chill, the smog, whatever
their reasons, along with those long-forgotten
slow-moving, fog-eyed houses, dew-jeweled lawns
leaf smells pungent as childhood
joys and anguish, as you come riding
to ball games, frog ponds, math tests, first loves, riding
legs and heart pumping, cresting a rise
to, gasping, let go, wind roaring, plunging
down the sweet curve of the Earth's breast, flying
out with the sun forever, atoms tingling,
into your life, before glass and steel
sealed you off, domed you, feeding you packaged bits
of the latest disasters, prices, hits
commercializing your options, blunting your sense
of miracles throbbing around you, but the birds
are still out there, singing
for anyone, free!

NEW AGE

Slowly, the overripe
season's
gold gown, skin

comes rustling
in tattered
majesty to the ground

and the long bone dream
of green
is everywhere.

LET'S PRETEND

"Dada, let's pretend
the floor is the water

and let's pretend
the water isn't dirty."

KITE
(for Colin)

1

All that rainy August we tried to fly
that lop-sided kite—an eagle
with a bum wing
that I kept trying to balance
with torn-off cigarette box tops.

I can still see you
heading into the wind
the kite rising behind you
circling crazily
then nose-diving back to Earth

or sitting half-hidden in meadow grass
the kite in your lap
watching me as I stood
at the other end of the string
in my raincoat, waiting for wind,
suddenly shouting for you
to hold it up and let go
then lunging, cigarettes spraying
screaming for you to come quick!

but by the time you'd arrive
the gust had died down
or the string got tangled in clover
or the box top blown off
or the rain started up again,
and you'd be hot and fed up
and want to go in.

The looks you gave me!
The looks I gave you back!

2

That was the same summer
I was attempting to launch
that insanely ambitious poem
about the evolution
and brotherhood of all things
in the universe,
taking it all the way
from the big bang
to a plea for future peace

struggling desperately
to breathe life
into lofty abstractions,
conceding that I was down
but never out

and finally finishing it
to no one's complete satisfaction
including my own

but defending it on the ground
that its vision was solid
important and clearly expressed
if nothing in soaring
to rival Rilke or Blake.

3

That was also the summer
you emerged as Batman

and I became the expert
on superheroes,
straining my hazy boyhood memories
for bits of Batlore
and making up the rest
whose many contradictions
you were quick to point out
like how could the Batcave
be somewhere out in the country
if Bruce Wayne lived in the city
and needed to get to the scene
of the crime at a moment's notice?

Hours and hours you spent
in your improvised mask and cape
trying to get your new image
off the ground,
flinging your Batrope's hook
up to the bars
outside the bathroom window
then clambering up the wall
halfway, suspended there
checked in mid-flight, but resolved
not to drop till your hands gave out!

4

Since then you've gone on
to Spiderman and other challenges
such as reading and learning to walk
by your hands across the top
of the backyard swing set

and my recent aerodynamics
in poetry
have involved the less cosmic

if no less high-minded realm
of humanity's need to set out
toward a new age.

We never did get that damn kite up
to stay,
but all those uncertain days
of common struggle
hope and disappointment,
illuminated by flashes
of partial success,
drew us closer together
than we'd been before

and may have helped us a bit
to see and accept ourselves
and our limitations
as fellow mortals
crashing as superheroes
while proceeding, anyway
in that lop-sided, crazy fashion
of human beings spreading
their dreams to the wind.

GHOSTLY VALENTINES
(for Danny)

Down on the high-school football field with you
toward dusk, still savoring the last trace of sweet
mid-February sunlight, it was cold!
I jogged in place, clapped my mittens, shivering
as I watched you climb the chain link fence, snagged,
   launched
the ball in a faint arc over the fading crossbar
at your blurred face, till my arm got sore, then raced
the length of the frozen field and back behind
your twinkling heels, having held back at first
unable to catch you at the end. Collapsed
on the hard dead grass, we lay panting, looking up
at silver taking the sky, the floating moon
hurled by some godlike hand, dark bony fingers
of trees, one clutching an empty nest. "I love
this time, the light, don't you?" I gasped, as we wheeled
our bikes together through the glimmering
hush of first stars and lit windows up the hill.
"Yeah," you huffed back, "and Dada, let's do this again
tomorrow, O.K.?" "O.K.," I said, "if there's time,"
doubting we would as we coasted home, our breaths
sending ghostly valentines back and forth through the
   dark.

WITH TENDEREST FEAR, RAGE, LOVE
(for Karen)

1

Wild gold spills down your back.
Woods stretch behind.
A field guide to my heart
held at your breast
your laughing eyes, teeth find me
through the lens,
a doe in lion's mane I stalked
with tenderest fear, rage, love.

2

Flowers pin half your hair.
Curled tresses lick your breasts
encased in white.
Stone at your back
you turn on the church steps
to smile at some congratulatory phrase
from the laced cage you stepped into
with tenderest fear, rage, love.

3

No silver threads
yet dull the crown you've woven.
Come from another meeting
you bend by the fire, working late
clusters of notes, toys, laundry, dreams
and drifting stars around you.
I put down my book, lie brimming, look
with tenderest fear, rage, love.

PROTHALAMION
(for Tom and Maxine)

Now, as before, and after
over and over
reach out and touch
the mystery of each other

feel how it trembles, swells
blindly pressing, yielding
in joy and terror
of giving, losing itself

holds back, while stretching
out to that savage, tender
twining of self and other
rooted, builds

a blossoming archway
that is both and greater
bidding you enter, together
the house of love.

FLOWERS
(for Amy Sophia Zuckerman
July 19, 1982—December 1, 1982)

We come bearing flowers,
fresh-cut, delicate blossoms,
which are all we have,
along with our tears,
to give

to you, who give more, blooming
inside us, insistent, coaxing
our arms round each other,
teaching us how
to live.

WINDMILLS

**(for George Abbott White, Ann Withorn,
and Gwyne Withorn White
on the occasion of the latter's christening,
June 18, 1983)**

Though my two-dollar poster copy
of Picasso's Don Quixote
keeps falling
flat on its sneaker-smudged
sun-bleached face
from a muggy wall
in my sweltering
junior high classroom

I keep stooping
to pick it up,
tenderly, lovingly
wiping it off
with damp paper towels,
and with little loops
of fresh masking tape
resurrecting

and sending the chronic dreamer
on his way,
grimed but undaunted,
singing, eyes heavenward, heedless
of Sancho's sputtered appeals
to reality,
armed with bright shafts
of June sunlight
that stab through the half-closed blinds

tilting at shadows, students
in their fashionably labeled
armor, moldering
grammar lessons scrawled
on the blackboard, headlines
from the President's latest
pitch for America

and whatever other
innocuous modern guises
evil assumes
that appear in his path
like windmills
to challenge him.

THREE TRIES AT A TOAST
(for Phil)

Here's to your first million by 40
your mug on the cover of *Time*
phone calls from Johnny Carson
and the White House
and the chance to refuse
an interview in *Playboy* . . .

Oh, that would be nice

but could you, who have chosen
your work from love of creating
beautiful things,
conquer the world, unstained
by its cutthroat power plays
for fame and fortune?

Then here's to the threadbare craftsman
of beauty, constantly driven
from dinner or bed to labor
in solitude
till the heart of his vision
flutters to life in his hands . . .

Oh, that would be nice too

but could you, who have chosen
a wife and a family,
be a slave to the muse
and honor the often mundane
demands of love,

fill pockets and cavities
with silver of inspiration
and cover the mortgage with dreams?

So here's to compromising
between those two tempting
stereotypes of success—
a toast from a fortyish
romantic, married, moderately successful
schoolteaching poet's heart:

may you fail to bring in that million
and still make a living from art.

ON SCHEDULE

By noon the rain that had been scheduled
to drift out to sea had thickened. Soon it turned
sleet gray, then more and more heavy flakes mixed in
till someone, looking up, announced, "It's snowing!"

Nothing much more got done all afternoon
or if it did our hearts weren't really in it
as we watched the world turn white, staring like cows
at magic quietly falling out of the sky.

Three inches later, at dusk, the stuff still piling,
the forecasters, their snowy feet in their mouths,
looking sheepish, anxious to salvage what they could
of their reputations, were calling for a whopper.

All evening by the fire we had visions
of being snowbound, sledding, making popcorn—
a day of grace when everything could happen
that our normal, busy schedules wouldn't allow.

Toward midnight, taking one last doubtful look
at the fairy maple, the sagging wires, the birch
that had nearly snapped in the blizzard three years ago,
we snuggled under the covers and fell asleep.

At four, trying to pinpoint what was wrong
I heard through the sifting darkness at the window
a steady, harsher pelting—refusing to look
at the senseless violation, I dozed till dawn

and dreamed of a girl in college I never slept with
who was saying goodbye; then played out several scenes
of things I'd scheduled for the coming day
and hadn't prepared for, each a tragic farce.

146

At six I met the maple's nakedness
head on, with a little sobbing laugh, went down
made coffee, glanced through the paper, and shoved off
for work, through a slush of dreams, on schedule.

A POEM ON SPRING
(for my poetry class)

This morning it was so nice
I took you out
into the late March landscape
still half-asleep, dreaming of green
in search of images
for a poem on spring.

"Listen!" I said, pointing
to a song sparrow in a bare bush.
"Look!" I said, bending
to a wall where dandelions
would bloom in a week or so.
"Come on, people, concentrate!"

But, clearly, we were too early
for the flower-crowned god,
and mostly we just wandered
the school grounds, chatting and joking,
glad to be out of the stuffy
classroom, in sun and air
with the moist earth under our feet
beginning to yield

though some of you took notes dutifully
and a few seemed inspired

and when I saw Lenny and Anthony
whacking a tree with sticks
like two woodland priests, after winter
rousing the sap,
I felt something stir, gather, rise

148

brimming over, as Mandy and Maribel
at the top of a hill
stretched out their arms and came whirling
round and around
down slowly toward me, beautiful
as any blossoms I've seen.

FRESH CAUSE FOR SONG
(for Isidore)

The poems you read
half-speech, half-singing
about being old and still
"the tree itself;"
your stillness, listening, head in hands,
as we took turns trying our own;
your eyes upon us, gentle as morning sunlight
coaxing a hidden animal, a leaf . . .

There's a picture I'd like to show you
in my wife's parents' house
of an old man out for a walk on a cloudless night—
he has stopped to admire the stars
and stands propped on his cane, when suddenly
taken with wonder, he sweeps his hat from his head
and greets the universe—in reply one star
comes tumbling into his bowler's upturned brim.

Old man, wearing so lightly
in what so often seems a darkening world
impeccable grace and courtesy
fresh as the cornflower in your buttonhole,
still turning up, at 82,
from the rubble of dreams and sorrows
that can choke a life
fresh images of delight, fresh cause for song.

BEARING WITNESS
(for Gary)

Imagine a world
with no one to stop and say
in a breathless whisper, Look
at that sky, that peak, that lake, that tree, that face—
how incredibly
vast, lofty, blue, brilliant, luminous
it is!

If nature means anything by us
it must have to do with this
beholding of wonders
and speaking them out,
that some creature stand up
to testify to the whole
unfolding wrought richness.

Others can stare,
can cry out in pain, terror, ecstasy
crow and keen,
but who else, gazing, can speak
words that move deeper
than sound, than light
into the dumb, mysterious
soul of a thing?

Imagine a world
silenced of awe forever, endlessly drifting
through the dim heavens, a speck
of flowering stardust
full of miracles, blossoming, passing
where no finger points,
no voice rises up
bearing witness.

BIG MEADOWS, Shenandoah National Park
(for Bill)

In the meadows at dusk, a sickle moon just starting
its long, slow swing through fields of ripening stars,
sparrows and doves send forth their drowsy hymns
to the last light, through air gone thick and sweet
with clover, clouds of yarrow. Ahead on the path
a shadow darts and rustles, becomes grass.

We search out the richer brown of grazing deer,
approach till their heads, still munching, lift and stare,
step closer, drawn till the invisible threads
of wonder and fear that bind us, tightening, snap
and they turn, leap, bounding away, the white flames of
    their tails
flashing, flickering, fading into the brush.

Somewhere deep in the encircling woods,
dark as a legend sleeping in our blood,
a black bear blinks, yawns, spreads enormous paws,
nuzzles her cubs awake, heaves from her den,
rears her majestic bulk to sniff the air
and rolls like distant thunder slowly toward us.

It is time to head back to campsite, lantern light . . .
still we linger, bending for one more handful of berries,
perching on boulders, our voices measured, low,
pointing out stars and silhouettes of trees,
then lapsing, mute, into the settling hush,
our faces featureless as worn, pale stones

our gaze spanning miles, millennia, faintly lit
with the gleam of hunters at home in the darkened land,
held for the moment somewhere in between
the ancient glittering mystery above us
and the far highway's muffled rush and roar,
the passing sweep and blaze of alien eyes.

MAYBE WE HAD TO COME THIS FAR
(for Irwin)

for this meadow
to pierce us
with such a rush of green

for this faint trickle
of life at summer snowline
to remind us how precariously
crawling we are
on the thin crust of the Earth

for these woods
cool and fragrant, still
with the hush of arrival
to refresh us so, offering
streams for our kneeling, berries
more precious than jewels

for these butterflies
busy with sweetness
resting a moment
unafraid, on our hands
to seem such an honor

for us to want so urgently
to fit in
taking our place in the landscape
as creatures among creatures
turning, not back, but at last
humbly, in praise
to the clear grace of water
the common gift of light